T0171438

Ten Keys to a Woman's Heart

A Book for Men About Women

Faith Richards

iUniverse, Inc.
New York   Bloomington

Ten Keys to a Woman's Heart
A Book for Men about Women

*Unless otherwise noted, Scripture quotations are taken from the HOLY BIBLE,
NEW INTERNATIONAL VERSION. NIV. Copyright 1973, 1978, 1984
by International Bible Society. Used by permission of Zondervan. All rights
reserved.*

*The views expressed in this work are solely those of the author and do not
necessarily reflect the views of the publisher, and the publisher hereby disclaims
any responsibility for them.*

iUniverse books may be ordered through booksellers or by contacting:

iUniverse
1663 Liberty Drive
Bloomington, IN 47403
www.iuniverse.com
1-800-Authors (1-800-288-4677)

*Because of the dynamic nature of the Internet, any Web addresses or links
contained in this book may have changed since publication and may no longer
be valid.*

ISBN: 978-1-4401-8574-8 (sc)
ISBN: 978-1-4401-8575-5 (ebk)

Printed in the United States of America

iUniverse rev. date: 8/6/2010

Acknowledgements

Thanks to those who read my manuscript,
supported and encouraged me.

Debra Brown

Marisol Morris

Katherine Kelly

Sandra Newman

Melissa Maulden

Diane Koceja

*To God
and this book to His Service.*

*To all men, especially to those who are of
the household of faith.
Galatians 6:10*

*To Bill
and the married men he represents,
who need Jesus and the principles
written herein.*

Table of Contents

Preface ix

Understanding A Woman's Heart 1

Getting Started 6

Step One   The Kiss 9

Step Two   Gift Giving 12

Step Three   Nonsexual Touching 16

Step Four   Dating 18

Step Five   Make Her Feel Safe 24

Step Six   Fill Her Love Tank 30

Step Seven   Living with Testosterone 37

Step Eight   Put Her First 40

Step Nine   Educate Yourself 44

Step Ten   Refuse to Look at Pornography 47

The Five Love Languages 51

Epilogue 57

Selected Reading 59

Preface

Ten Keys to a Woman's Heart is short and to the point. It's for marriage veterans with years of experience and those just entering a relationship who don't have a clue. This book is not a sex manual. Nor is it a quick fix. It's a guide to a woman's heart.

The answer to a more fulfilling marriage isn't taking her away for a long weekend or planning a romantic dinner. It goes much deeper than that. The patterns that both of you have fallen into may need to be broken and remade. Sound too much like work? I guarantee the results will be worth it!

Wouldn't it be great to have a satisfying sex life–really satisfying–instead of just one step beyond self-gratification? Isn't it your heart's desire to have your wife look at you with respect and admiration? If you answered "Yes" to either question then you've picked up the right book. Your happily ever after is only pages away. Let's get started!

Understanding A Woman's Heart

Who are you in your spouse's life?

- Her protector?

- Her provider?

- Her lover?

- Her safe place?

God called you to be each one of these things. It's summed up in His command for husbands to love their wives.[1] Many men today have no idea how to do this. Marriage to them is just a coexistence because they weren't taught any different or had no example to follow.

By incorporating the following steps into your everyday life, you'll get a woman who responds to you. One who eagerly looks forward to your home coming, who loves you with all her heart,

---

1 Ephesians 5:25

and who'll never leave you. Sound too good to be true? Meet the needs of her heart, gentlemen, and she'll be yours–freely, willingly and gladly!

At first the process may seem like an uphill battle but don't quit! Especially if many years have gone by of the same old, same old. She may have built up some walls but they can be penetrated with tenderness and patience.

Guys, please get this. We respond to how we're treated. That's how God made us. A woman has needs too–emotional ones–which are often disregarded by men. Because of this, women have learned to become like camels. One good drink (metaphorically speaking) sustains them for a very long time. If you doubt this, think of how long your wife can go without sex.

The truth is most women are thirsting for true love and affection. By sincerely nurturing this side of them, the maintenance is very little. A smile, a kiss, or a touch reminds them they're loved and cared for.

Every woman wants to feel beautiful and be cherished. It's an innate desire that God put inside each female. Many women read romance novels, watch chick flicks, and yes, soap operas, to fill this need vicariously. For them it's a temporary satisfaction of a deeper longing. A yearning that's awakened as a young girl the first time they hear the story of Cinderella, Snow White or Sleeping Beauty.

This is one reason why so many women are taken advantage of by smooth talking Romeos. These men know what works, but for them it's just a superficial means to an end. Not so for you. As you read, you'll learn how to gain a stronger and deeper connection to your spouse than you ever thought possible. You will learn the keys to her heart.

Heathcliff Huxtible, of The Bill Cosby Show, knew the value of knowing his wife. In one episode, he and his two sons-in-law had a contest to see who could do the best job at winning their wives' hearts. The catch was they could only spend twenty-five dollars to do so.

The newly wedded son-in-law bought his wife a sterling silver tube, a time capsule for their fiftieth wedding anniversary. The first entry was the stem from the flower she wore in her hair during their honeymoon, which he had saved in a handkerchief.

The eldest's spouse, Elvin, gave his wife a silver strand bearing three pearls. The pearls represented their marriage and two children. He told her that each year on their anniversary he would add one more.

These men were indeed thoughtful but Heathcliff knew his wife. He teased Claire about the hair comb she wanted years ago when they were dating. (He didn't have the money to buy it at the time.) She became visibly upset as he started to describe another girl's hair clip. Claire vividly remembered the exact size and color of the one *she* wanted. When she tore open the box, it was exactly as she'd described much to her chagrin. Heathcliff sat there beaming. He had won.

Now on the flip side, let me tell you about a personal experience. My family had lived in Georgia just six months when my husband got called out with the National Guard to be backup for the 24th ID in Desert Storm. Thinking he wouldn't be able to share Christmas with us, my son and I went to spend the holidays with relatives in Tennessee.

When I heard my spouse had a chance to come home for Christmas day, I drove twelve hours straight, four of which were in a snow storm, with my three-year-old son. Nine hours into the trip we were involved in a car accident but still managed to make it home late Christmas Eve. I also stopped in South Carolina to get my husband's favorite fireworks, so I wouldn't be empty-handed on Christmas morning.

The next day, exhausted but happy, I watched my son and spouse open their gifts. I looked forward to opening mine but received nothing. Not even any kind words about coming all the way home.

My husband had missed a perfect opportunity to touch my heart. A special card. A piece of jewelry to wear while he was away. Something! Anything! Needless to say there was no sex that night. But you can bet Bill Cosby's character got some.

Guys, these stories show that with a little effort on your part, we can all get what we want. Unless you are an insensitive oaf or an abusive male, you should be able to see that women are like beautiful, long stemmed roses. Strong, yet fragile. Our feelings, like the petals, can become easily bruised. You're probably at a total loss as to why, so let's move on to provide you with understanding and skills.

Getting Started

First, let's discuss why the magic has gone out of your marriage or for the newly married, how to keep that special spark. Do you remember how you scored points in the early part of your relationship with the gifts you gave her for no special reason? Or how she responded when you told her she was beautiful and her eyes drove you crazy? Those words and gifts were filling a part of her that only you could and she responded in kind because you were reaching her heart.

Why doesn't she respond anymore? Because you quit saying and doing the things that fed her spirit. She stopped seeing and hearing how much she meant to you. Oh, you think she should know that by now. Do you still want sex after all this time? Well, she still wants tender talk.

It's a huge turn on for a woman to hear how much her partner wants her. (Wants *her*, not wants sex.) She loves knowing that she excites him. A woman will risk being vulnerable if she feels secure in your love. How do you help her feel more secure? By telling her and showing her over and over how much she means to you. Don't let it just be part of your lovemaking but of your everyday life.

What do you say or do before you leave in the morning? Do you let her know by a kiss, a smile, or a word, that you'll miss her? These simple gestures make her feel special. They help to keep you on her mind. However, some women may need more.

How does your spouse react when you talk about her body? Does she brush you off when you tell her how great she looks? Believe me, she's hearing you, however, she may doubt you mean it.

Insincere words cause pain. Everyone's been there, done that, and has the scars to prove it. Wanting to believe what someone says in order to fill a need is different than believing them because they truly care. Some women have been so wounded that developing trust may take some time. Don't take it personally. Be patient. Only say things you mean and she'll learn to accept them. And don't overlook those "three little words." Women can't hear them enough.

One summer I asked the men I worked with if they ever called their wives to tell them "I love you." You should've seen their faces! For those of you who haven't said it in a while, you might need to take it slow. Your spouse may wonder what you're up to, like some of their wives did.

The best present you could give to your children is to love their mother. You're also setting an example for your sons. If all goes well, they won't need a book to teach them how to love a woman. They'll learn by watching you. And make sure to tell your children you love them too, at least once a day.

Step One

The Kiss

Ah . . . the kiss. What's in a kiss? Passion, love, friendship? Do you remember the oldies song, "It's In His Kiss"? It's true. A woman can tell a lot about a man by how he kisses. Is he stingy with his kisses, sloppy, in a hurry? Or does he take his time to kiss and kiss well?

The same old boring thing is just that, boring. Have you kissed the same way since high school? Then it's definitely time for a change. On the way home from a road trip, my college boyfriend and I decided to pass the time trying out different styles of kissing. (We weren't driving.) It taught me there's more than one way to kiss and I've never forgotten it.

Kissing is an art and it *can* be learned. It's also fun! And nothing but nothing, gets a woman ready to make love like some good kissing. So, learn, baby, learn.

Feel the softness of your partner's lips, chew on them, and kiss them one at a time. Feeling the moistness of her mouth is delightful, but this brings up an important point. Swallow! Swapping spit is as exciting as it sounds. And please use a breath mint if you think you need one.

Kissing is also interesting after drinking something extremely hot or cold. Enjoy the sensation and one another. Explore. Be playful. It'll become serious business soon enough.

How do you get to that point? Look into her eyes and proceed to kiss her softly and slowly, (without laughing.) Passion is sure to follow. One reason is because you're taking your time. Letting her know she's worth it.

Want to score big points? Kiss her and don't push for anything more. Instead, hold her face, feel her hair, or if you're standing, hold her hands, intertwining fingers. She'll feel loved and cherished, and that's the feeling you're going for. It may be difficult but it'll be worth the effort.

After implementing these suggestions, her sexual desire will definitely increase. There isn't a woman alive who doesn't want to be kissed and held. Learn the art of kissing and she'll be putty in your hands.

TIP: Don't swallow her face! Match lip to lip (that's where the nerve endings are.) Take turns playing follow the leader. Letting her lead will show you what she likes.

Step Two

Gift Giving

The easiest and sometimes most heartfelt gift you can give is a card. Stores carry them for all occasions. All you have to do is agree with what they say. This can come in handy if you have a hard time expressing yourself. Cards are especially welcomed when they are given for no special reason. Ones that say "I'm sorry" tucked into a grocery store bouquet will stop the continuation of any argument at the door!

When buying a gift, use your common sense and observation skills. If you're shopping for jewelry, think about what she already wears. Necklaces, rings, bracelets, earrings, funky pins? For instance, if her jewelry box is full of gold, you wouldn't buy her sterling silver.

Does she like big pieces of costume jewelry or delicate necklaces? Charm bracelets make a good gift. They come in different sizes and materials. Rope bracelets usually include one charm or a disc to engrave; larger loop chains and solid circles can hold many charms. There's even a watch band type.

Once she has the bracelet, you can always add a single charm commemorating something special, making it a truly thoughtful gift. One man I know got his wife a heart charm for Valentine's Day, but instead of putting it on a bracelet, he took her shopping for a necklace. And yes, there is more than one type of chain.

If all this is foreign to you, check out the jewelry kiosks at the mall. But don't be intimidated. Gift giving isn't rocket science; it just takes a little bit of know-how. You can always go into a jewelry store and ask the clerk for help. And if your spouse doesn't accessorize with jewelry, there are always watches.

If clothing is more appropriate, check out her closets and drawers for the right sizes. Never go into a store without knowing her size or her favorite color. Notice what styles she wears, and then combine it with what you like. If lingerie is more your kind of gift, get a Victoria's Secret credit card and go shopping together. It's more fun that way.

Challenge yourself to know your wife's sizes from top to bottom. I guarantee she knew yours before the honeymoon was over. There's nothing wrong with buying something sexy, but no thongs unless she already wears them. Most women either love them or hate them. However, if you go for feminine and comfortable, it probably won't be taken back.

Perfume, fragrant candles, or collectibles also make good gifts. Women seldom splurge on themselves, so why not buy her favorite scent in a gift set or large size? And if she likes to collect bunnies then anything with a rabbit on it becomes an "aww" gift.

Let the kids give the practical presents. If she really wants a new mixer, have little Eddie give it to her, not you. Remember your goal is to touch her heart. Family holidays such as Christmas, Easter, and Thanksgiving don't have the same emphasis on romance as Valentine's Day, an anniversary or birthday.

Leave Mother's Day to the kids, but make sure you have a token of appreciation. A gift certificate to a spa, perhaps? A time of pampering is one gift a woman will never return. But make sure she picks out the services or it may backfire. She may think you're telling her she *needs* a facial, a pedicure or a bikini wax.

If you're a flowers kind of guy, why not try different varieties? There are now so many kinds too pick from in grocery stores. You can bring home a beautiful bouquet or buy a vase if it's a special occasion. If you aren't sure what to buy, ask a florist for advice. Find out if your spouse has a favorite flower and make sure there are many of those included in any bouquet or arrangement you choose.

Most women think a dozen roses cost too much. One long stem rose is romantic. Six are sweet. Or try knocking us off our feet with two dozen. Then tell us we're worth it. Miniature roses are also beautiful and not as expensive. (FYI roses come in colors other than red.)

TIP: Don't wait until the last minute. Don't buy her candy if she's dieting. And don't buy her exercise equipment (as a gift) under any circumstances! Trust me on this.

Step Three

Nonsexual Touching

Is there really such a thing as nonsexual touching? Absolutely! It's that touch on the shoulder or kiss on the head that leads to nowhere. A touch that means nothing more than I love you and appreciate you. Holding her hand while watching a movie, playing with her fingers across the table at a restaurant, or a quick massage of her shoulders while she's cooking dinner, are all examples of nonsexual touching.

Nonsexual touching includes *not* touching the sexual areas of her body, i.e. no grabbing the butt! A woman needs to know she's not just a sex object to you. Playing with her hair, stroking her arm, kissing a shoulder, all let her know you're there and you care.

You can't go wrong with the three H's. Hugging, holding, and helping. They feed a woman like a three course meal. Hugs are comforting, especially after a long day. They say "I've missed you." And a great hugger never pulls away before the other person.

To be held in bed at night provides a sense of security that paid bills and house alarms just can't match. Spooning is also great. Another fun way to be held is to have your spouse lean back against you and let her wrap your arms around her like an old sweater.

Some guys think all this touching stuff is boring, but it's actually one more step toward your goal. So quit being so selfish, loosen up, and you just might enjoy it. If your spouse's love language is physical touch, this is not an option!

The third H is helping. This means taking out the trash or putting away the dishes, making the bed, changing a diaper or giving the children their baths. Don't say all she has to do is ask. It's your house, too. A timely act, totally focusing on what she needs at the moment, may be the most heartwarming thing you could do.

Helping touches her in the same way as hugging and holding. It's foreplay for the mind and heart. The three H's show by your actions that you care and that can't be reinforced enough.

Step Four

Dating

Let's start with what dating is not. A date is not a stop for fast food. It's not a grocery shopping trip. It's not a bite to eat after visiting a major home supply store. And a date does not include the kids. It is made for the sole purpose of spending time together.

Too many couples consider going out to eat after an activity, a date. They usually have nothing to say to each other throughout the meal. If you're at this stage, it's time to start the rebuilding process.

What did you like to do together when you first met? Was it a picnic in the park or camping? A walk on the beach, a night out on the town, or pizza and a movie? The whole purpose of dating back then was to spend as much time as possible with the other person.

What activity would make her eyes light up again? The answer may take some thought but that's okay. If you're a marriage veteran of a decade or more, it's probably been a long time since you've done something just for the sake of being together.

Why do married people feel they have to stop acting like they're in love? Is there a maturity rule that kicks in after so many years? It was fun then, it can be fun now.

Maybe you've gone to the movies lately. But how long has it been since you leaned over and kissed her during the show or purposely got that back row seat so you could have some privacy? Oh, you came to watch the movie and *like* sitting down front.

Has life got you so preoccupied, that you forgot how much you enjoyed your spouse? You've committed the rest of your life to this person, so why not enjoy it? The following is a strategy for getting back into that mind set. It's as simple as a trip to the mall.

Oops, there goes half of you! Calm down. Your purpose isn't to shop but to get to know your wife better. How many of you really know your wife's likes and dislikes? Here's a chance to learn some new things about the person you sleep with every night.

Ask her what her favorite store is and take her there. If money was no object, what would she buy? You might be surprised at the answer.

Go to a clothing store or a shoe store and ask her to show you what she likes. Pick out some things you like and see what she says. Don't worry, guys, you won't be there all day. This is for informational purposes only; she's not buying.

Make it interesting. Go to the evening gown section of a department store, pick out something you like and have her try it on for you. Next go to a lingerie shop and do the same thing. Although modeling there might not be a good idea. The point is to have fun. Take your time. See what she likes and store it in your memory bank for later. Afterwards, sit on a bench and people watch.

Guys, I didn't say girl watch. Don't blow it here. Be sure to hold hands as you sit together or walk through the mall. The only person you're trying to impress is the woman at your side.

Finally, eat at one of the nicer restaurants to end the date. You'll be surprised at the conversation you'll have as a result of such a stressless time together. Then next week go back to the mall by yourself and get one or two of the things she liked, as a surprise. You will score big points.

What may seem uncomfortable in the beginning will turn out to be enjoyable. It'll delight your wife to know that you want to spend time with *her*, instead of catching up on other things. A woman misses that, and sometimes she misses you when you're standing right in front of her. You're creating desire in your wife by letting her know you like being with her. You're backing your words with action.

For the next date, try something that you're both absolutely no good at, like bowling or miniature golf. How about going to a driving range, a batting cage, or maybe try skydiving? She'll love the vulnerable quality that you'll exhibit by attempting something new. The world is your oyster; experience it with the one you love.

After doing this a couple of times, you'll be ready for more traditional dates. Try to date about twice a month. If you choose a movie or bowling, don't forget to bring a little flirting into it. For example as she bowls, make a comment on how much you like the view. Lean over and kiss her neck in the movie, or take her to a drive in and steam up the windows. If she brushes you off, it's too early. She still needs time to see if you're sincere.

Your spouse wants to know if you really want to be with her, or if it's just temporary insanity. If the needs of her heart have gone unmet for very long, it may take time to rebuild that trust. But be patient; it'll happen.

After a few months of "practice" dating, you'll be ready for the romantic date. Everything you've done so far has been leading up to this point. The last step is to sweep her off her feet. If you'd tried this cold, it would've been just another dinner date. By cold I mean without all the preliminary dating. What you've done is laid a foundation.

A romantic date can be as simple as a meal (cooked by you) followed by dancing in the den. Leave the dishes and take her hand, curl it into your chest, and use the other hand to pull her close. No woman would turn down a night of slow dancing by candlelight. You can buy small votives and candleholders anywhere. It shouldn't cost more than $20 for both and they're reusable!

Another suggestion is an evening snuggling on the couch to watch a movie together (after the children have gone to bed.) Take into consideration what she would like to watch and pick a movie with that in mind. She might even surprise you later by sitting through one of your "shoot 'em up" dvds. You could also use the votives here and watch the movie by candlelight.

Now you're ready for the formal date. Make reservations at a nice restaurant or go to a show, (not a movie.) Buy her a dress to wear. After all, you know her size now. Take pride in looking good and smelling good and don't forget the flowers!

For those of you that might need an audio visual aid, try the Andy Griggs song, "(All Week I've Been Your Husband) Tonight I Wanna Be Your Man." If you watch the video, you'll understand how by doing these things, you'll both reap the rewards.

TIP: Hold all doors open for her, including the car door. This is something that should always be done, not just on a date. And if you don't already, make it a habit to put your napkin in your lap at restaurants. Do this as soon as you sit down and you won't forget.

Step Five

Make Her Feel Safe

How a woman reacts is in direct correlation to how secure she feels. Insecurity does not feel safe. It breeds a lot of ugly stuff, including nagging, jealousy, anger, and fear. That's why it's so important to tell a woman you love her. Those words provide security.

When a woman's security is threatened she can stress big time. Whether it's unpaid bills, the loss of a job, or simply an argument. How do you make her feel better? It's often as easy as taking her in your arms and telling her everything's going to be alright.

Remember those men in the old black and white movie classics that kissed a woman in mid argument? *They* knew what to do. Even if the woman's pride made her resist at first, it wasn't long before she'd succumb to his kiss. Why? Because women *need* that reassurance. It's part of their nature. That kiss and/or hug says, "No matter what happens, I love you and will take care of you." Such security is extremely conducive to romance.

The Bible tells us God took a rib from Adam to form Eve.[2] What's the significance of that? The ribs protect the vital organs. It's a word picture of how man was made to protect a woman and especially what? That's right, her heart. You're to be her covering, her protector, her emotional bodyguard.

In a marriage ceremony, the father transfers the responsibility of his daughter to the groom by placing her hand in his. By doing so, the father and the bride put their trust in the new husband. But the person she trusts the most can also hurt her the most.

Remember when you promised never to break her heart? How many times since then has she cried? Probably too numerous to count. Well, believe it or not, every time that happened, she closed off a piece of herself to you. Why? Self

---

2   Genesis 2:21-22

preservation. If she doesn't feel protected *by* you, she'll feel she has to protect herself *from* you.

Some of you are beginning to understand your wife's behavior for the first time. You're starting to see why walls have grown up between you. But do you know you helped build those walls brick by brick?

There's a measure of safety behind barricades no matter who erects them. Yet the Berlin Wall showed the world that no matter how thick, any barrier can come down. In marriage, one way to break through is a good heart to heart talk.

Try not to let the distractions of the day get in the way. Don't try this during dinner, with the kids around, or in a public restaurant, and definitely not in bed after a long day. A preferable time to talk would be after a good meal. Sneak off to a part of the house with a neutral and relaxed atmosphere, like the den.

Sit opposite each other with knees touching. This position helps to promote intimacy while talking. Look into each others' eyes, making an effort not to look away. Take turns talking for five minutes each, less, if you don't need the full time.

Taking turns is a great way to get a point across without raising your voice. The knee to knee position may also be necessary if you or your spouse have a problem with interrupting. It provides neutral ground. Holding hands is also a good idea. (It prevents you from crossing your arms.) Touch communicates that what you're saying is important.

Another area a woman needs to feel safe is in the area of finances. Money problems are rated as one of the top reasons for divorce. It needn't be if men would assume their leadership role. Believe it or not, most women aren't cut out emotionally to be the bill payers.

It's your job description as a husband and leader of the family to make sure the finances are in order, that there's supply instead of lack. Many women prefer to take on the bills because they need to know (trust) that things are being paid on time and the lights won't go off. Many men have fallen short in this area.

Even though women may take over the finances, it's not the correct order of things. Men need to take back this responsibility. Women are the engineers of the home. They manage, plan, and direct the operations of the household, even if they're employed full time. Men are to monitor and provide for the supply and demand.

If you truly feel you're not good at financial management, ask God to help you. He's great at checks and balances; look at nature. Seriously, it may take a while, and your wife may balk a bit, but stand firm. You can do all things through Christ.[3]

If she has a system, learn it. She'll watch you like a hawk at first, but her respect for you will double, once she sees she can trust you. Without that extra burden, she'll go to bed a more peaceful woman, and much more open to romance than when she was wondering how the bills would get paid.

Another important money matter is a joint banking account. If you don't have one, get one. Separate checking accounts are not conducive to oneness. If you need to feel some autonomy, how about separate savings accounts? Each person decides how much they put into it every pay period. The rest is pooled together.

Always make major monetary decisions together. If things get tough, don't complain to her. Pray. God is the supplier of all your needs and

---

3   Philippians 4:13

the lifter of your head.[4] This doesn't mean hide things from her. Be honest but also be reassuring. Remind her of the promises of God. Teach her about the steadfastness of the Lord and she'll translate it into your faithfulness to her.

---

4   Philippians 4:19, Psalms 3:3

Step Six

Fill Her Love Tank

When children are growing up, it's the parents' job to make sure their love tanks are full. Full love tanks develop good self esteem and trust. In marriage God commands the husband to leave his father and mother and cling to his wife[5] so, the job of filling her love tank continues on as his.

So, exactly how do you this? The first way is relatively easy. Compliment her. In the same way men need admiration and will do almost anything to get it, women will respond to a sincere compliment.

One of the ways to a woman's heart is through what she hears. Words can be used to bless her or curse her. The words spoken (or not spoken)

---

5   Ephesians 5:31

through the years directly affect how your wife responds to you today.

What you say doesn't alter who she is, but it does change how she feels. Don't mistake filling her love tank for building her self esteem. Filling her love tank makes her feel loved and secure. That's your job. It's up to God to teach her who she is in Him and how valuable a person she is.

Do you remember how your bride blushed when you told her how beautiful she was, or how much she meant to you, or how much you loved her? Why do those words of love and affirmation disappear over the years? Well, when the romantic dust settles and everyone gets comfortable, a routine is often formed.

A kiss before bed or saying I love you before hanging up the phone is great, but a woman needs more. She's like a sponge, soaking up everything, positive or negative. Her sponge-like ability doesn't differentiate. A woman's vulnerability to her spouse is affected when more negative than positive is absorbed.

Picture a water tower. Every time it rains the water level rises. Each time the water is run, the level goes down. After a while with no rain and constant depletion of this resource you have what's called a drought. What was once in plentiful supply is now limited and restrictions are put on its use.

It's the same with a woman. Praise and affirmation raise the level but constant criticizing or lack of *rain* lowers it, to the point of unresponsiveness or discord. Sometimes an attitude of indifference develops because she doesn't feel special anymore. That doesn't mean this is a right attitude. In fact the Bible says just the opposite.[6] But it may be a reason why your wife sometimes acts the way she does.

Compliments and praise are not to be confused with flattery. The Bible says flattery is deceitful and used only for gain.[7] Women, especially your wife, will know when you mean what you say and when you don't. Some women have lived on empty for so long that they won't believe anything you say or on the flip side will compromise themselves in order to hear a few kind words.

For women, giving compliments comes naturally. They're the nurturers. It's not that easy for men. Men feel they must *do* something to gain admiration, whereas, it's not in a woman's

6   Luke 6:28

7   Romans 16:18

nature to do something to get something. That would be considered manipulative.

Men seek the prize. They're the conquerors and expect kudos for their accomplishments. When men don't receive respect at home, they find it in other places. That's one reason why so many men are workaholics and/or have affairs. It's a vicious cycle where nobody wins. But with some effort on your part you can learn how to sincerely love your wife with words. Remember, women are responders. So, by filling your wife's love tank both of you can get what you need.

The second way isn't so easy but it's possible. Become best friends. This doesn't mean she takes the place of your male friends. But she is your wife, your life partner. She should be privy to information that no one else knows. So, share your heart with your wife.

Nothing builds intimacy better than being vulnerable enough to show your weaknesses or share your doubts and fears. Unfortunately, most men feel like the following: "Me? Show my weaknesses? On purpose? No way! I don't want anyone to know I have weaknesses. Men are supposed to be strong."

Nope. Seeing her hero stumble once in a while makes him human. It's endearing and she'll guard that knowledge fiercely. She feels special when you're real with her. That's the key.

Another way to fill her love tank is by making an effort to remember the "little things." Men aren't as tuned into the opposite sex as women are. Women will know and remember how you like your coffee before the first date is over. They also take for granted that you aren't into the details like they are, so by becoming more observant, i.e. studying your wife, you'll score big points.

The same goes for talking things out. Even if your wife's concerns don't seem very important to you, make an effort to listen to them. Discuss them with her. Be a sounding board. All she may need is verbal reassurance and a hug.

The Bible says to love your wife as you love yourself.[8] Do you honestly think of her as your equal? Do you give *her* feelings the same credence as your own? *That* is loving her as you love yourself.

Deep down many men have the opinion that women aren't the weaker sex but the lesser. It takes a mature man to realize otherwise. If you're willing, God can de-program this and any other faulty thinking. Just ask Him.

---

8   Ephesians 5:28

Speaking of feelings, please don't tell your wife, or your children for that matter, to feel or not feel a certain way, or that their feelings are silly. Feelings are as involuntary as heartbeats. They come and they go. You can't stop them or create them. Your only choice is how you act on them. Let your wife know that her feelings are important to you and she'll feel loved and valued.

Experiencing intimacy with your spouse is a great way to fill both your love tanks. It's feeling that special connection. A private moment only the two of you share. One way to create this is by praying together.

Two becoming one takes place as you go to your Maker in one accord. (And you thought that only applied to sex.) Make it a daily habit. Find the best time for both of you. This is not family Bible time or personal devotions. It's a time for the two of you to join hands, literally, and speak to your Heavenly Father.

A daily devotional for couples could get you started in the morning. Or if you're a night person, have prayer time right before going to bed. (This prevents anger from being carried over to the next day.) Or do both. Whatever is best for you, but do it religiously!

Don't let anything get in the way of this special time. If you're apart for some reason, pray over the phone. Praying together will shed love abroad in your hearts in a whole new way. God's way. Agape love.

Always take the time to come together in prayer before making big decisions. Turning things over to your heavenly Father brings peace. Surrender and humility go hand in hand.

"Pray without ceasing," Paul says.[9] Even though he wasn't married, I believe he would've made it a point to pray with his wife. This isn't an excuse to forsake your own time with God. You must have both. Seven days without prayer makes one weak and a target for the devil, so remember to also bind the enemy together. For one may chase a thousand but two put ten thousand to flight![10]

---

9   I Thessalonians 5:17

10   Deuteronomy 32:30

Step Seven

Living with Testosterone

Someone once said that a man's sex drive brings him back home each night, but the lack of it in a woman is what keeps her faithful while he's away. I asked the Lord one day, why He gave testosterone to young boys. It seemed unfair to unleash this powerful hormone on unsuspecting young men. The answer I received was amazing.

Testosterone was needed to complete man's character, to teach him control. Man would have to make very tough decisions and learn to say no. (Think how different things would be if Adam had done this.)

Even after the fall, God expected man to lead his family. This male hormone would teach him how. As an adolescent is guided by his parents into adulthood, his Heavenly Father also prepares him through this man drug.

Man's struggles with testosterone are the equivalent to a woman's flux of emotions due to estrogen (or the lack of it.) Like a woman's menstrual cycle, testosterone has been blamed for everything, but that wasn't God's plan. Testosterone wasn't meant to be a liability but an asset. A man who's able to bypass his natural impulses for the greater good is a man who's not only in control of himself, but an effective leader as well. This is true in business *and* marriage.

It's said that a man thinks more with his penis than with his brain. This is because the majority of men let themselves be controlled by this hormone. They think only of how to satisfy their wanderlust.

Some women use this to their advantage. They know how to tap this reservoir to get what they want. These women use men, just as men use women, but hopefully your wife, or wife to be, isn't one of them.

Have you allowed this male hormone to control *you?* If so, ask for a crash course in godly control. Training to become the man God intended you to be, as well as the husband your wife wants and deserves.

A woman needs a man she can respect and a man in control of himself is always attractive to the opposite sex. In the same way children need boundaries to make them feel secure, your wife may need to depend on you to draw the line when she can't. To know she can trust her husband and his godly decision-making process is worth more than gold.

Step Eight

Put Her First

A woman needs to feel that she's the most important in your life. She wants to believe she's at the top of your priority list. In her mind she gave up everything to become yours. She'd like to feel that you did the same. After all, she could've had anybody but chose you. Sound familiar?

Nothing can bring discord to a marriage faster, than a woman who feels you love something more than her. A woman doesn't want to compete for your attention. She'll nag you instead.

To some men, life revolves around golf or going out with the guys. To others, it's sports. To a lot of men, work takes up the majority of their time. This includes working at the computer. The key is to enjoy these things without leaving your wife on the sidelines. A woman can get downright aggressive if that's the only way to get your attention.

One way to get what you both want is to sit down and talk about it. It may be you need to take a break from your beloved activities in order to show her that she *is* important to you. Your willingness to do so may be all she needs. (Reassurance that she didn't marry the wrong one.)

Another idea is a contract. A written or verbal *agreement* on time spent away from one another. That way both of you can pursue what makes each of you happy. (And for those who might try to include a romance clause here–don't push it.) Hopefully, you're not enmeshed in a relationship where she believes she needs you in order to breathe. For that you'll have to seek professional help.

Doing things that you enjoy, add to who you are. Just don't give these activities such importance that it puts your wife on the back burner. After all you married *her*!

My husband liked to hunt. I didn't. I didn't mind him going. I knew it was a good outlet for him but sometimes I wanted to make plans during hunting season.

A good wife knows to do this sparingly, but one who doesn't feel secure will try to get her way.

Why? She wants attention. The less attention she receives, the more arguments you'll have. "If you loved me, you wouldn't work so much . . ." "Why don't you sleep with your *car* then . . .?"

There's a simple way to fix that. Think of us *first*. Before you play golf, leave us at home with the kids, or stay at work late for the third night in a row, talk to us. Ask about *our* plans for the day or if you need to bring home dinner. Check with us for scheduling conflicts. In other words, don't be so self centered! Be a little more flexible and considerate.

If women feel they're first on the priority list, they'll have no problem in letting you participate in the activities you like (or in rewarding you for coming home on time.) When you do come home, share with your wife some of the things that happened that day, funny or exasperating. That way she becomes part of it and doesn't feel left out.

There's always the option to bring her along. Well . . . who knows? It might turn out to be fun. But ask her only if you mean it. You wouldn't ask your wife to join the company bowling league but she might enjoy watching you bowl. At least she'd be happy you asked.

All she wants is to be considered. Most women enjoy the time alone. Just don't leave them alone too often or they may start wondering about your activities.

In summation, talk to her about the things you like to do. Work with her if there's a conflict. Checking in at least once during your absence scores bonus points, even if it's to tell her you're on the way home. You may actually experience more freedom in the long run by giving up a little now. Everybody wins!

Step Nine

Educate Yourself

By educating yourself I don't mean go back to school. The title simply means to make yourself more knowledgeable. I've already suggested to my son that when he becomes engaged, he read up on how to satisfy a woman. I want his married life to be a happy one.

Education goes both ways. It wasn't until my separation that I started reading about how to please a man. I used the Internet. No, I'm not telling you to look at porn. That topic is covered in the next chapter. The Internet can be a *good* source of information. I typed what I wanted to know in the search engine and found valuable articles and great how to's. This is perfect for those of you who aren't book readers. (That's why I made my book short and to the point.) I learned something and you can too!

Your love life may be one area of marriage where the spark needs to be rekindled. Most men seem to have the same, repetitive way of doing things, and it used to be wives never said a word. Times, however, have changed. Same old won't cut it anymore.

Women don't want to feel like a depository. Maybe not all women, but most would agree they don't want to be viewed as sex objects. They don't want to be objects at all. They're people.

Sex with your spouse was made to be a coming together. In the physical sense, it's the closest you'll ever be. Spiritually, it symbolizes oneness. It's not an act–it's an experience!

Sometimes men have to work a little harder at making sex a selfless experience. A woman likes a slow, caring approach. Not to say fast and furious isn't as much fun.

Fun! That's the key word. Make your time together enjoyable! Pray about your sex life. God is a great resource for creativity and inspiration. *He* gave us the ability to orgasm.

Don't separate the experience in bed (or wherever) from the rest of your marriage. Foreplay starts in the morning and continues all day, even while you're at work. A call, a caring act, a kiss on the neck when you get home, makes a big difference in how you'll be received that night.

Please do not tell your wife goodnight, turn off the light, and then plant a hand on her body that is supposed to let her know what you want. Use your mouth! (Verbally or nonverbally.) The grope in the dark is so annoying. Some guys even have the nerve to try this after an argument. For those of you who really don't know—bad idea.

This isn't to say forego the romantic interludes in the middle of the night. To be slowly aroused during the night (pun intended) is a wonderful experience. One suggestion—try it without words. Afterwards, go back to sleep as if nothing happened. Tremendously sexy.

One last tip is to watch a show on the Discovery Channel called *Berman and Berman*. They're sex therapists who have a very matter of fact style, and they get results. After watching a show or two, include your wife. She may hesitate at first but she won't for long, as it really is interesting. Who knows? If you've done everything you've read so far, she may be up for some discovery of her own.

Here's your challenge. (Yes, this whole book is a challenge.) If you've got what it takes, start reading the covers of women's magazines in the cashier line and even buy one or two. Not for your wife, but for you. As Jeff Foxworthy says, "It's like spying inside the enemy camp." Learn about her. Teach her. Love her. You know you don't want to live without her!

Step Ten

Refuse to Look at Pornography

Pornographic sex is totally unrealistic. It's fantasy; yet, it can destroy marriages. Pornography continues the objectification of women by reducing females to body parts made for pleasure. It lowers women's self esteem by degrading them to mere playthings. Your wife is a person. An equal.

This may be Step Ten but it's importance ranks much higher. If you want to keep pornography in your house in any form, you might as well toss this book in the garbage right now.

From the wife's standpoint, a husband looking at pornography without her is like an act of betrayal. Something or someone else is arousing to him. Using pornographic material isn't the way to fill a need. What you *need* is to consider her feelings on the subject.

Pornography puts unrealistic expectations in your mind. It brings competition into the bedroom, which your wife will never be able to meet. It affects her body image and self esteem. She knows she can never look like those girls and therefore feels less than.

Viewing porn on the computer is like playing with fire. It's totally addictive and leads to nowhere fast! Would you mess around with cocaine? Oh, you don't do drugs? Well, lust is a drug. A powerful one. Take a tip from Joseph and flee from any form of it![11]

Another way it's similar to drugs is that it's progressive. What starts as a curious interest in the female form usually doesn't stop there. This *interest* is what keeps you going deeper and deeper.

What the world is privy to by a click of a button leaves one in awe. Fetishes, bestiality, and S & M (Sado-Masochistic behavior) are just a few. There are even chatrooms on these topics and more. Chatrooms lead to relationships and relationships can lead to affairs, emotional and/or physical. Stay away from them! They're like roaring lions waiting to devour you.

---

11 Genesis 39:11-12

Check out what *looking* did for David. Not only did it lead to adultery but also to murder.[12] He later wrote in Psalms 51:9 "Create in me, O Lord, a clean heart and create a right spirit within me." You can ask God to do the same for you.

David also vowed to the Lord to set no vile thing before his eyes.[13] That's a motto to not only put near your computer but on the television as well. Why do parents tell their children they can't watch certain things? They're protecting them. Adults need to learn to protect themselves as well, by watching what they drink in with their eyes.

This book is about the keys to a woman's heart. Pornography isn't one of them. It's a relationship *killer*. There's a BIG difference between educating yourself and using pornography. If the difference isn't clear to you, ask God to reveal it.

---

12 2 Samuel 11

13 Psalms 101:3

The Five Love Languages

It's time to discuss a very important aspect of getting to know your wife. Her love language. According to Gary Chapman's book[14], there are five.

- Words of affirmation

- Physical Touch

- Acts of Service

- Gifts

- Quality Time

There's an easy way to find out which language is hers. People have a tendency to complain when their language isn't being spoken. What does your wife nag you about the most? See if you can match these phrases to the appropriate love language.

---

14 *The Five Love Languages,* (Moody Publishers, 2004)

- "You never spend time with me!"

- "I'd appreciate some help around here!"

- "Why don't we ever hold hands like we used to?"

- "You never say anything nice to me anymore."

- "It's Valentine's Day and you come home empty handed again."

Imagine the joy when spouses have the same love language. They give and receive what nurtures them the most. However, most times opposites attract. God made it that way so we could complement one another. The talker needs a listener and the shy person needs a more outgoing partner. This is also true of love languages.

Nurturing your partner's love language may not come naturally to you but you have to try. This helps to fill her love tank. Speaking her love language brings satisfaction and contentment to your spouse. The following is a brief description of each love language for your understanding.

Words of affirmation are compliments and/or praise. Some people need to *hear* others affirm them, i.e. they're doing a good job or they look especially nice. As they receive these words, the level in their love tank rises. This isn't to be confused with self esteem. How you see yourself comes from the inside. When someone is speaking your love language you feel loved. Kind words are to an affirmation person what caressing is to a physical touch person.

Men who aren't used to giving compliments and have a wife with this language need to start praising her daily. One man kept a note on his dashboard reminding him to do so. And heaven forbid, don't forget those three little words with these women!

Many men think their language is *physical touch*. But they mistake the wanting of sex for this love language. Physical touch people enjoy hugs and hand holding. They usually incorporate touch into their conversations. They may also be very particular about the kind of material they wear next to their skin.

If you think your wife may have this language, the next time you are alone try picking up her hand and kissing her finger tips or sucking the sauce off her fingers when you eat barbecue ribs or chicken.

Physical touch people are forever hugging their kids and *always* rock their babies to sleep. They tousle hair, kiss goodnight, rough house and tickle, which is great for the children in the family that also have this love language. So, if you come from an "untouchable" family, you're very likely to starve your wife in this area if you don't start reaching out, literally.

Gifts people are the easiest to please. They appreciate anything you give them. From the smallest flower to the largest bottle of perfume, it doesn't matter. Gifts make them feel special and the fact that you thought of them makes them feel loved.

Those with the gifts language also enjoy giving. People usually demonstrate their own language. Gifts people never miss a birthday and their favorite holiday is Christmas. If this is your wife or child, make sure you plan a good birthday celebration *every* year and don't ever come home from a business trip empty handed!

Remember when I said in Step Three that changing a diaper might be the most heartfelt thing you could do for your wife? This is true for *acts of service* people. No amount of touching, gifts, or nice words will make them feel as loved as finishing that project, taking the garbage out, or pitching in at bed time.

For some reason these are the women who get stuck with the couch potatoes or sports enthusiasts. Getting their husbands to mow the lawn or even change a light bulb is a hassle. It must be that opposite thing. If you put forth a little effort here and her tank is full (as well as the car) she'll love you for it.

In this fast paced world and busyness of life, the last love language can be the hardest to nurture. Women with this language want your time, *quality time*. They don't want to be pushed aside or postponed. It's important to them that you do what you promise.

This type of woman needs tender loving care, in person. Taking long walks (you don't even have to hold hands), making it home in time for dinner, or quiet talks when the kids go to sleep, all help fill her need for quality time.

If this is your wife's language, it's imperative you find time to spend with her. Nothing else you do will make her as happy.

People that aren't nurtured in their individual language live on empty. That's why when parents give their children material things, it doesn't make them feel loved unless their language is gifts. Or if you find yourself saying, "You don't appreciate anything I do," your wife is not an acts of service person, but you are!

Husbands that are hard workers and good providers are most appreciated by an acts of service wife, while the gifts wife still wants him to stop and get her flowers on the way home. The physical touch spouse wants a big hug as soon as he comes in the door, and the affirmation spouse wants to hear that he missed her. The quality time partner is just glad that he's home.

So, find out which language fits *your* wife. She may be more than one. Most people have a primary and a secondary language. While you're at it, love your children in their own unique language. And don't forget to let your wife know what *you* are, although it's a good bet she already does.

Epilogue

Well, hopefully you're not too overwhelmed. This *is* a lot to absorb. Dive into it whole hog (ol' southern expression) or take it one step at a time. The latter is probably the best method. If you sincerely put these principles to work, you'll have a better relationship.

At first it may seem like you're doing all the work. However, you're dusting off old techniques that used to make her happy and incorporating new ones. The work doesn't stop after you do it once. This is a lifestyle change–for the better!

You'll have fun working the steps and you'll definitely be having fewer arguments. *That* has to be worth something! Plus you receive the bonus of getting to know your wife in a whole new way.

For the woman it starts in the mind. First she'll notice the little things you're doing. Then once she has the time and attention she so desires, you'll start seeing a change. Why? Let's say it together. *Women are responders!*

God bless you on the road to a happier destiny with the one you love. Always remember to make it a threesome—you, your wife and Jesus. For God said, "It is not good for man to be alone." Genesis 2:18.

Selected Reading

The Five Love Languages by Gary Chapman – How to express heartfelt commitment to your mate. (Moody Publishers, 2004)

If Only He Knew by Gary Smalley – A valuable guide to knowing, understanding and loving your wife. (Zondervan, 1997)

What Wives Wish Their Husbands Knew About Women by Dr. James Dobson – Suggestions for marital happiness that are interesting, practical and humorous. (Living Books, 1981)

Maximized Manhood by Edwin Louis Cole – Being a man is a matter of choice. This book is about that choice. (Whitaker House, 2001)

Every Man's Battle by Stephen Arterburn and Fred Stoeker – Winning the war on sexual temptation one victory at a time. (Waterbrook Press, 2003)

I Love You but Why Are We So Different? by Tim La Haye – Understanding your spouse's temperament, with its strengths and weaknesses, makes for a happier marriage. (Harvest House, 2002)

His Needs Her Needs by Willard F. Harley Jr. – Building an affair-proof marriage. (Revell, 2001)

How to Give Her Absolute Pleasure by Lou Paget – Explicit techniques every woman wants her man to know. (Broadway, 2000)

Love and Respect by Dr. Emerson Eggeriches – The love she most desires. The respect he desperately needs. (Thomas Nelson, 2004)

The Holy Bible – All scripture, inspired by God, useful for teaching, rebuking, correcting and training in righteousness. For the man of God to be thoroughly equipped for every good work. 2 Timothy 3:16

Amazon.com provides a description and review of each book. *You may order additional copies of this book through iUniverse.com and other online bookstores.* May the Lord direct you on the path to a more fulfilling union!

God bless,

Faith Richards
Psalm 37:4

Certificate of Appreciation

*Given to First Class Husbands
Who finish reading this book in its entirety,
And courageously endeavor to make
the changes needed
To live happily ever after.*

On behalf of wives everywhere—Thank You!